The ChattyMe

Journal

Naomi Wilkinson

For my boys.

May you continue to talk to me about everything.

This journal belongs to

_____

So What is The ChattyMe Journal?

We all know how IMPORTANT it is to eat lots of healthy food and do some exercise every day, but did you know it's just as important to have a HAPPY healthy mind? That's where this journal comes in. Here at **Chatty HQ**, we believe we should talk about everything; our dreams, our favourite memories, our fears, and even what makes us angry. We want your ChattyMe Journal to be full of your fun doodles, awesome ideas and fantastic thoughts. But we also want it to be a place where you can reflect on some of the not-so-good parts of your day too. We all have days where we feel sad, anxious or angry but so often we don't talk about it and it builds up and builds up until we EXPLODE! These big feelings need some BIG ideas as to how we can react and deal with them...

1

Felix and Harper

Meet Felix and Harper. They live amongst the pages of your journal and can't wait to tell you all about their days! They might need your help sometimes too.

Felix
Favourite food: chocolate ice cream
Favourite colour: green
Best day out: seaside
Biggest fear: shark attack

Harper
Favourite food: pepperoni pizza
Favourite colour: purple
Best day out: theme park
Biggest fear: thunder storms

All About Me

My name is:_____

I am _____ years old

Here is a picture of what I think I will look like when I'm 20!

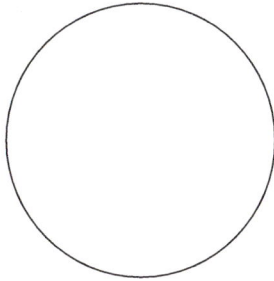

Favourite food: _____

Favourite colour: _____

Best day out: _____

Biggest fear: _____

Picture of favourite animal:

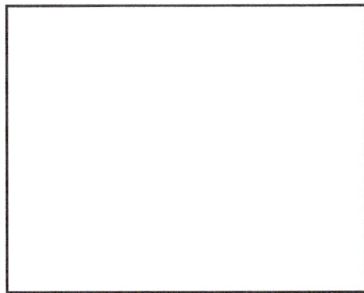

Any brothers or sisters? _____

Dream job: _____

Big Feelings

Everyday we feel different feelings. We might wake up feeling calm but a rain storm on the way to school makes us feel frustrated. Then we get our homework back and we've got a fantastic mark, which makes us so happy, only to find out in maths that our favourite teacher is leaving, causing us to feel sad.

It can be a constant rollercoaster ride up and down, happy and sad, EXCITED and anxious. Some feelings last a long time, others maybe just for a few minutes. We all love feeling happy and excited, but we are not so keen on feeling sad or anxious. We don't like how it churns our stomach into knots, makes us feel sick, or makes our heart beat really fast.

4

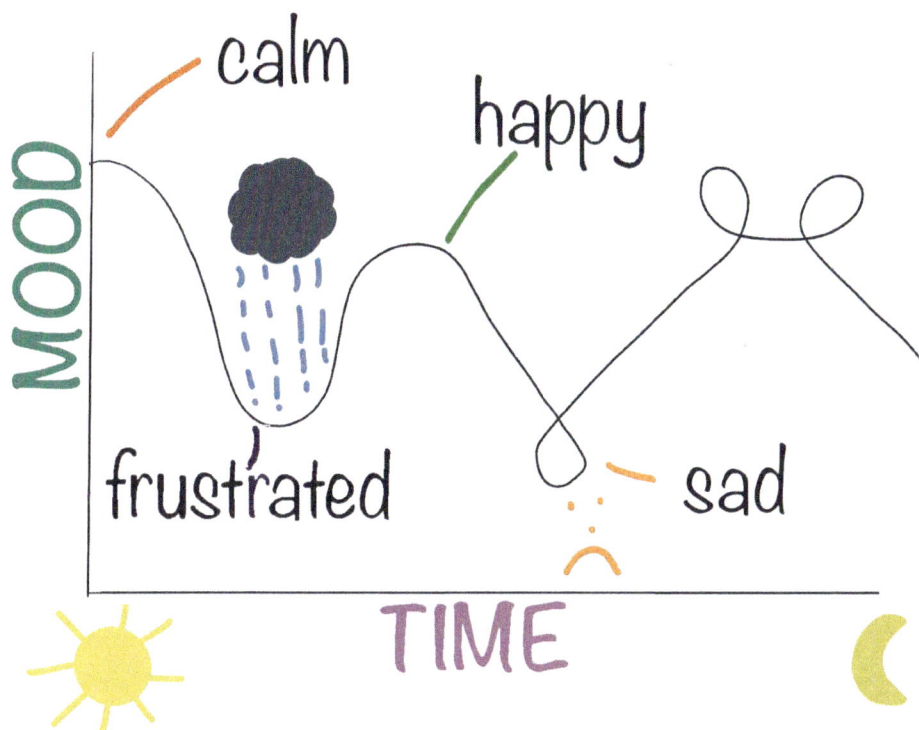

Sometimes our feelings get so BIG and scary we need a bit of extra help to work out what to do with them. So how can we deal with these big feelings?

Anger

Felix loves playing tennis, but absolutely HATES losing! He gets so angry and erupts, a bit like a volcano. But what does anger actually feel like?

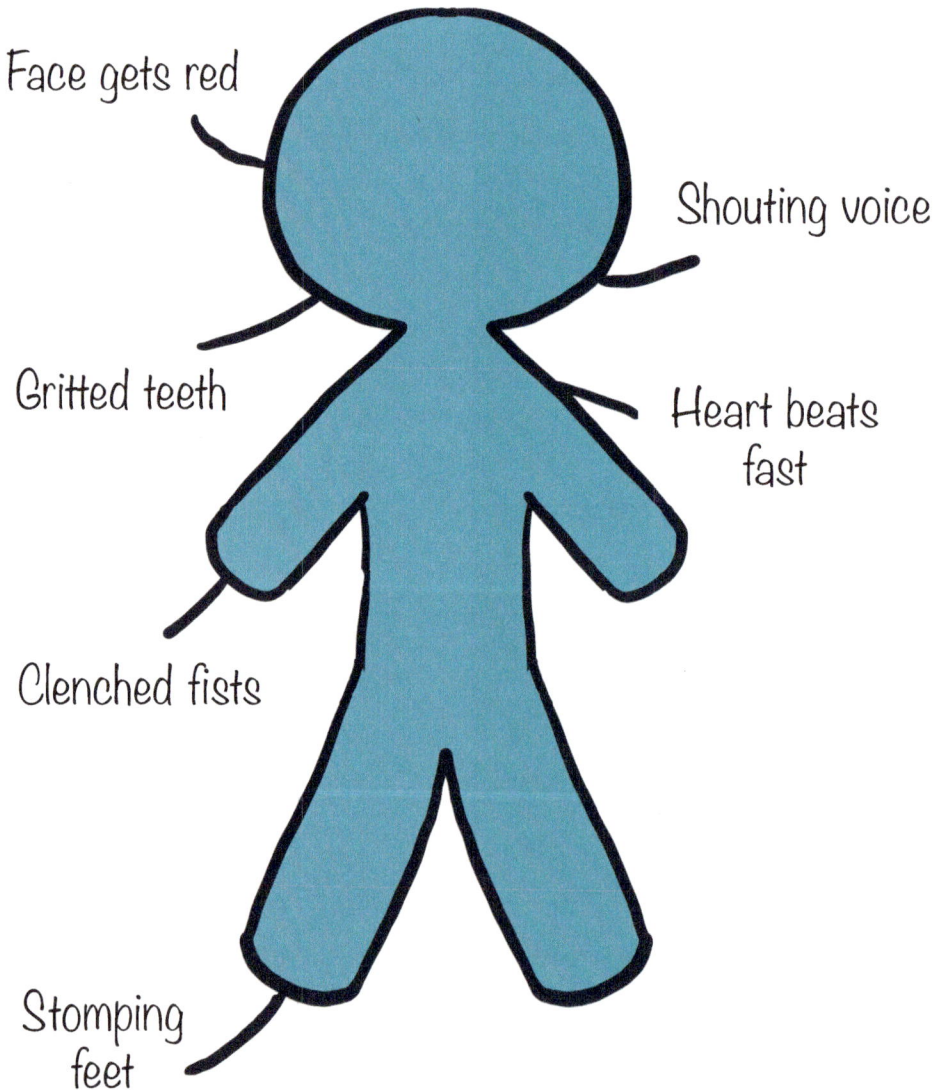

Face gets red

Shouting voice

Gritted teeth

Heart beats fast

Clenched fists

Stomping feet

How can Felix deal with this big feeling? Look at the tools in Felix's anger toolbox. Can you add any of your own?

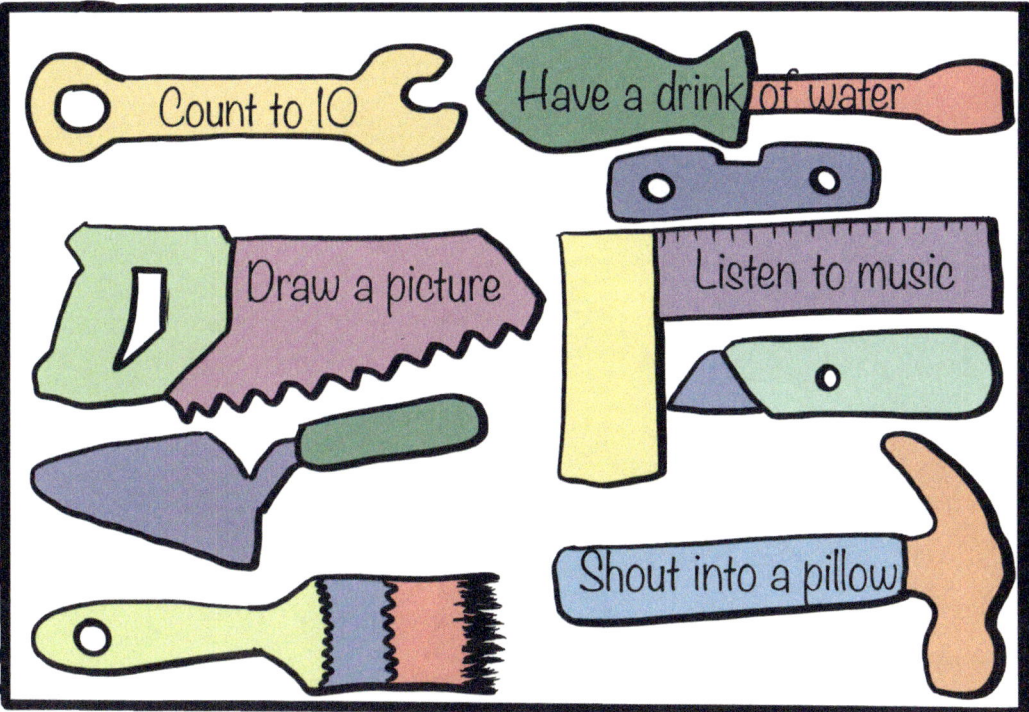

Count to 10

Have a drink of water

Draw a picture

Listen to music

Shout into a pillow

Which tools will you use next time you're angry?

Sadness

Harper feels sad because she has lost her favourite toy. But what does sadness feel like?

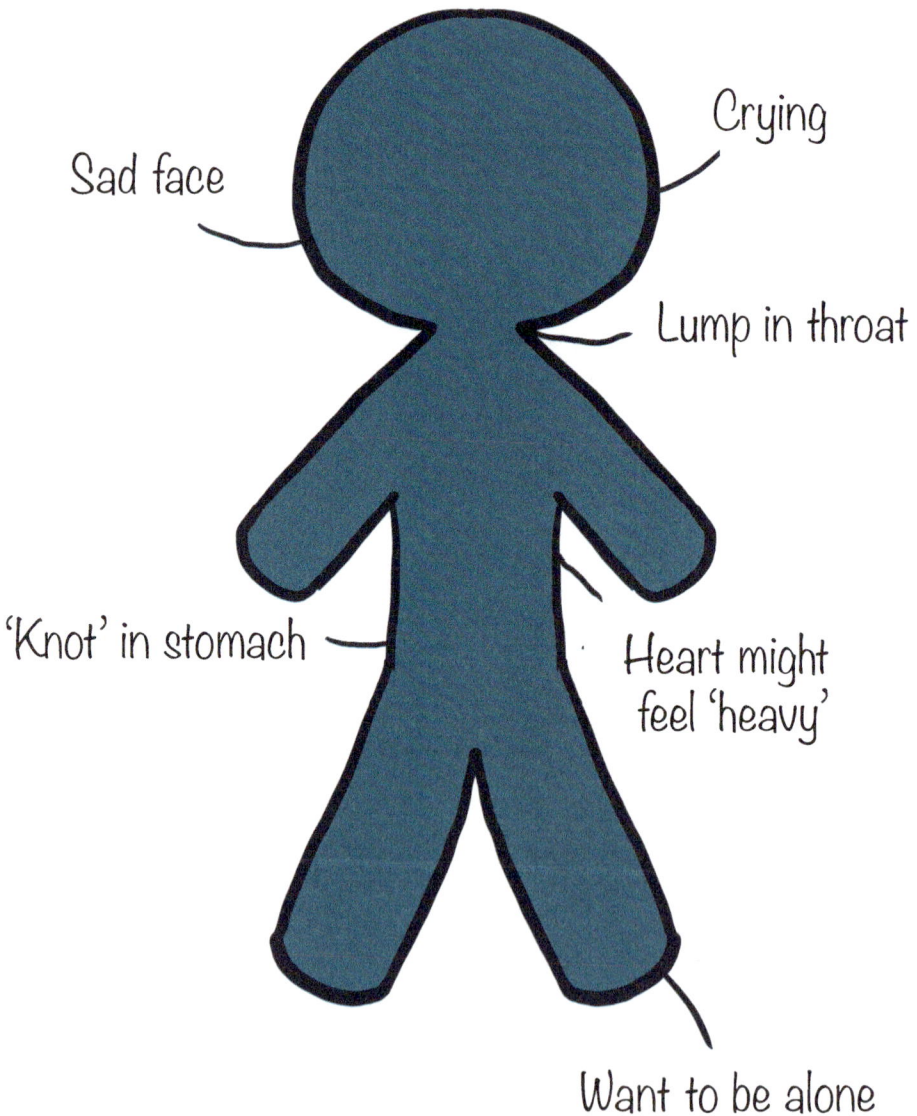

Sad face

Crying

Lump in throat

'Knot' in stomach

Heart might feel 'heavy'

Want to be alone

How can Harper deal with this big feeling?
Look at the tools in Harper's sadness toolbox.
Can you add any more?

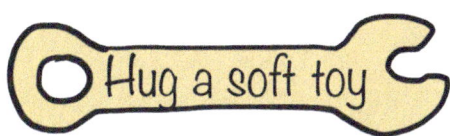

Hug a soft toy

5 things you're grateful for

Chat to a friend

Play at the park

Draw a picture

Watch a movie

Which tools will you use next time you're sad?

Anxiety

Felix feels very anxious when he has to try something new. But what does anxiety feel like?

Negative thoughts in head

Bad dreams

Sweaty palms

Heart racing

'Butterflies' in tummy

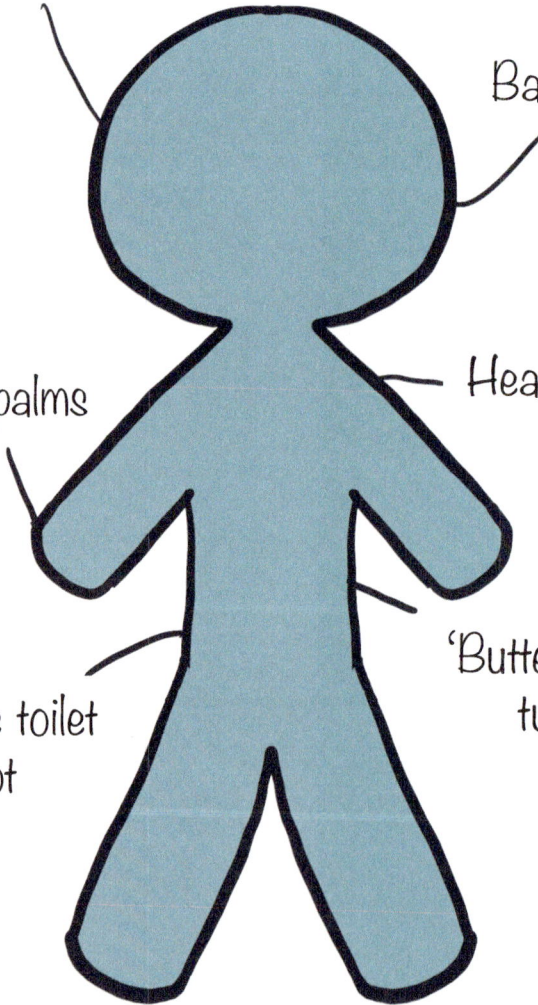

Need the toilet a lot

How can Felix deal with this big feeling? Look at the tools in Felix's anxiety toolbox. Can you add some more of your own?

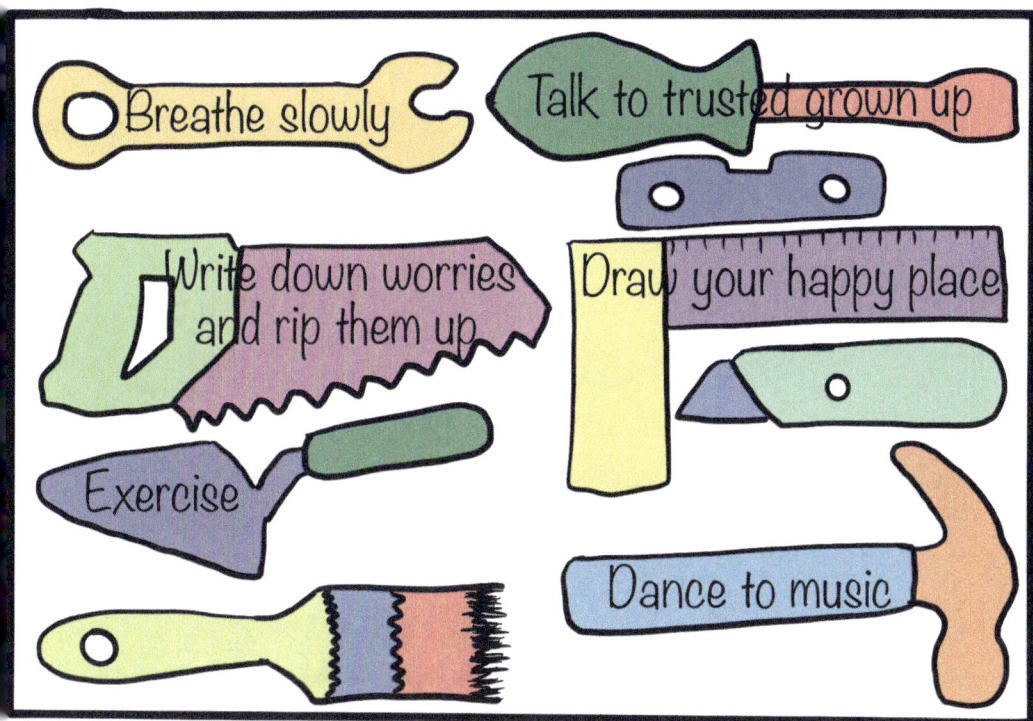

- Breathe slowly
- Talk to trusted grown up
- Write down worries and rip them up
- Draw your happy place
- Exercise
- Dance to music

Which tools will you use next time you're anxious?

Mirror, Mirror On The Wall

Take a look in the mirror. What positive things can you say to yourself today?

I am amazing

I am helpful

I am loved

I am kind

I am a great friend

I try my best

I am brave

I am enough

I am a good listener

I am creative

I am important

I make good decisions

I am free to be myself

I am special

I am unique

Choose one from the list every day and practise saying it. Colour each one in when you really believe it about yourself!

Heart to heart

We have so many things in our lives to be grateful for; what makes your heart happy? Write or draw as many wonderful things as you can think of.

Fill up your tank

Imagine a big tank in your body. When our tank is full, we are calm, happy and positive. When our tank is running low, we feel sad, tired and anxious. We need to keep our tank filled up throughout the day by having time to do fun and relaxing things, but different things can make our tank get low. If we're too tired, have too much work to do or someone is mean to us, it can empty our tank. We call filling up our tank, 'self-care'. Everyone has to practise self-care, even grown ups. This might be meeting up with friends, having a nice bubble bath, chatting on the phone to Grandma or even going on a bike ride.

Can you think of some things that would help to fill up your tank? Write them in the tank now, and remember to do them often.

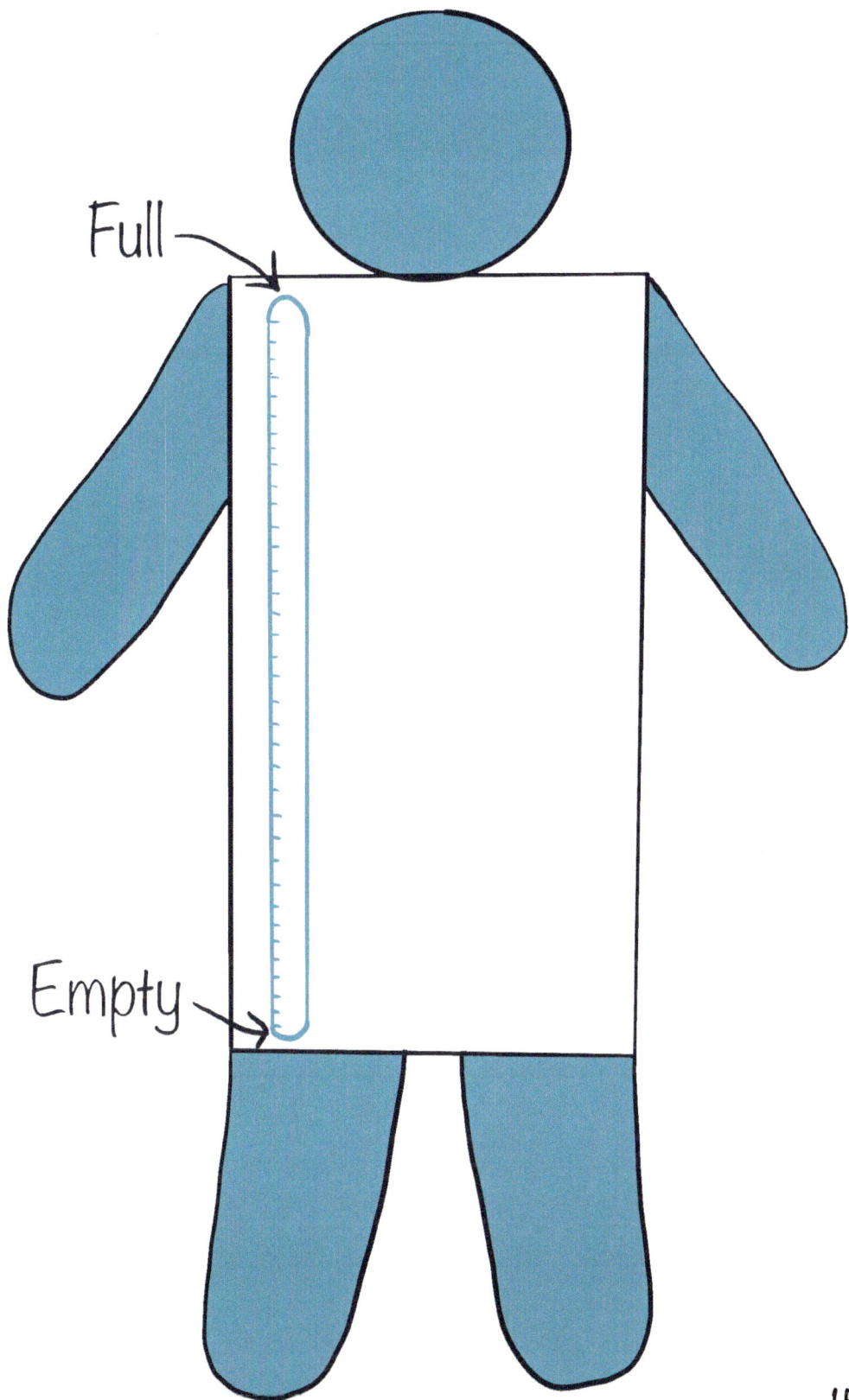

Full

Empty

A-Z

Can you think of a word to describe you, starting with each letter of the alphabet?

A   N

B   O

C   P

D   Q

E   R

F   S

G   T

H   U

I   V

J   W

K   X

L   Y

M   Z

Colouring Page

Pop on some relaxing music and enjoy this colouring page.

My Favourite People

My Favourite Things

I Love Me!

Everyone at Chatty HQ thinks you are AMAZING! What do you think makes you so awesome?

Journal

So, are you ready? We're about to launch into the world of ChattyMe, and we can't wait to have you on board! Each day is undated, so you can start whenever you want and fill your journal in as often as you like; every day, four times a week, or just at weekends. The choice is yours. The most important thing is you have fun, learn something new about yourself and chat about all of your feelings.
What are you waiting for?!

Date: _____

Draw how you feel today on the face.

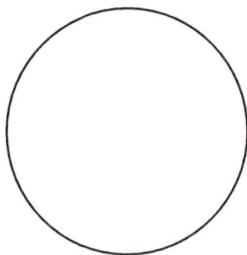

What was the best part of your day?

_____

How were you kind today?

Tidied my room ☐
Shared my toys ☐
Helped in the kitchen ☐

_____
_____

Harper is going to a friend's house tomorrow.
How do you think she feels?

Day 2

Date: _____

Where are you on the happy-o-meter today? Draw a picture of you on the line.

_____

O - Sad   5 - Ok   10 - Happy

Has anyone said anything kind to you today? Write it in the speech bubble and let it make you smile.

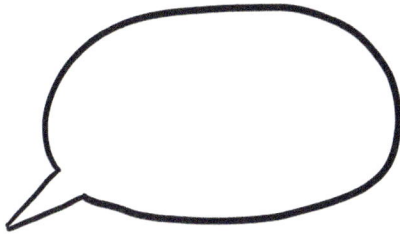

One thing I have learnt today is: _____

_____

_____

_____

Felix has lost his maths homework.
How does he feel?

23

Date: _____

How does your heart feel today? Colour it in using the key:

Happy Angry Calm

Excited Anxious Sad

Did anything amazing happen today?

_____
_____
_____

One brave thing I did today was: _____

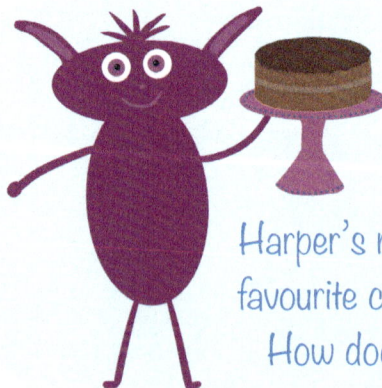

_____

_____

Harper's mum made her favourite chocolate cake. How does she feel?

Day 4

Date: _____

How do you feel today?

_____

Did anyone help you today?

_____
_____
_____

Draw 3 things you're excited about.

Felix fell over and cried today. Has something made you cry today?

Day 5

Date: _____

Write an acrostic poem to describe 'TODAY'.

T
O
D
A
Y

What was the most exciting part of today?

_____
_____

Did you notice anyone feeling sad today? How did you help them?

Hugged them ☐
Sat with them ☐
Helped them to find
a grown up ☐

_____

Harper had such an exciting day at the farm today. Where's the most exciting place you've ever been?

FARM →

Date: _____

Circle all the feelings you have felt today.

Sad   Anxious   Calm

   Happy
                        Angry   Excited
Other_____

Did anything happen to make you anxious or worried today? _____

_____

How can you help someone tomorrow? Draw it here.

Felix is so excited! It's his birthday next week. What are you excited about?

Day 7

Date: _____

3 best moments from today:

_____
_____
_____

Draw something you found hard today.

Was anyone kind to you today?_____
_____
_____
_____

Some children were being
mean to Harper at the park.
What should she do?

28

Day 8

Date: _____

Fill in the faces to show how you felt at each part of today:

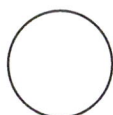 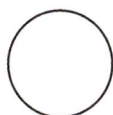 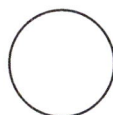 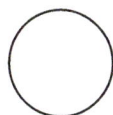

Get up   Lunch   Dinner   Bed

Did anything surprising happen today? _____

_____

_____

If you could go anywhere right now, where would it be? Draw it here.

Felix got angry today and threw lots of toys on the floor, breaking his aeroplane. What tools can he use from the anger toolbox on page 7?

Day 9

Date: _____

What were the two best parts of today?

        1. _____

        2. _____

What did you do that was creative today?
Can you draw it?

If you could redo any part of today to make it better,
which part would you choose? _____
_____
_____
_____

Harper really wishes
she could be
invisible for a day!
What superpower
would you choose?

30

Day 10

Date: _____

How are you feeling right now?

How are you feeling right now?

What was the hardest thing you did today?

_____

_____

How can you make tomorrow even better?

Do more exercise ☐   Watch less TV ☐

Go to bed earlier ☐   Help prepare dinner ☐

Offer to tidy my room ☐   Be kind ☐

_____

Last year, Felix went on a tour of some
really old caves, and loved it.
What's the most interesting
thing you've ever done?

Day 11

Date: _____

What score would you give today out of 10? _____

What has made you smile today?

_____

What are you looking forward to tomorrow? Circle it, or add your own.

Going to the park

Seeing friends

Baking a cake

Reading a book

Watching a movie

_____

Harper isn't well enough to go to her cousin's party. How does she feel?

Date: _____

Draw your favourite part of today.

Think of something you know today that you didn't know yesterday. _____

_____

What did you do today to take care of yourself?

Have a bubble bath ☐   Go to the park ☐

Watch a movie ☐   Catch up with friends ☐

Go swimming ☐   Learn a new skill ☐

_____

Felix has a spelling test tomorrow and feels very anxious. What tools can he use from the anxiety toolbox on page 11?

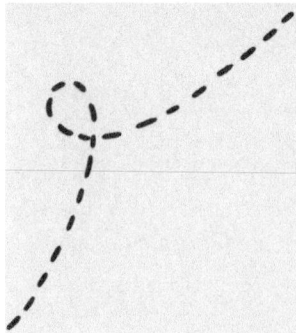

DOODLE PAGE

DOODLE PAGE

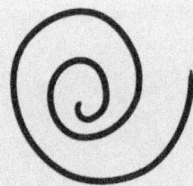

Day 13

Date: _____

Draw how you're feeling today.

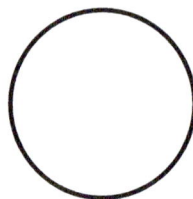

○

Think of one thing that went well today and one thing that could have gone better:

Went well: _____

Could have gone better:_____

What has been the proudest moment of your life?

_____

_____

Harper loves having family
movie nights. What special things do
you do with your family?

36

Date: _____

What was your favourite moment from today?

_____

_____

What are you most proud of yourself for today? Colour in your answer.

Helping cook dinner

Being kind

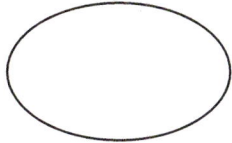

Being brave

Learning something new

Finishing homework

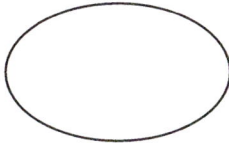

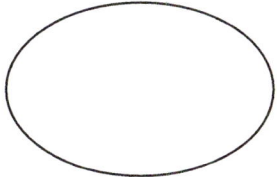

When is the last time someone upset you? How did you react?

_____

_____

_____

_____

Felix's best friend is going through a tough time at school. What can he do to help him?

37

Day 15

Date: _____

What feelings have you felt today? Add your own if you need to.

Sadness   Anger

Happiness

Excitement   Anxiety

Did you struggle with anything today? Draw or write it here.

Finish this sentence: When I'm finding something hard I will..._____

_____

Harper loves painting. What are some of your hobbies?

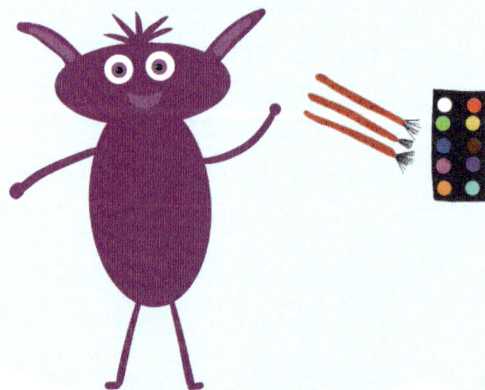

Day 16

Date: _____

Name 3 things you are grateful for today:

_____

_____

_____

Have you learnt anything new about yourself today?

_____
_____
_____

What are you most looking forward to tomorrow?

_____
_____

Felix loves building robots at weekends. What is your favourite thing about weekends?

Date: _____

Use 3 words to describe today:

1. _____
2. _____
3. _____

Draw something that made you laugh today.

What did you struggle with today? _____
_____

Harper taught her
sister how to bake cookies. What skills
can you teach someone?

Day 18

Date: _____

Draw your favourite part of your day.

Did anything happen today that upset you?
A friend was mean ☐
Got pushed over on the playground ☐
Lost at a game ☐
Not allowed a second cookie ☐

_____

Is there anything you are
anxious about tomorrow?

_____
_____
_____
_____

Felix had a really good
dream last night. Have
you had any dreams recently?

Day 19

Date: _____

Write each letter of your name down the left side. Can you think of something that happened today starting with each letter?

Did anything make you anxious today? Can you draw or write it in this space?

How could today have gone better?

Got up earlier ☐
Eaten a healthy snack ☐
Spent more time outdoors ☐
Chatted to a friend ☐

_____

_____

Harper has lost her bedtime cuddle bear. How does she feel?

Day 20

Date: _____

Circle all the feelings you have felt today

What was the best part of your day? _____
_____

If you could learn any new skill, what would it be? Use the ideas, or add your own.

Piano ☐   Sky diving ☐

Goalkeeping ☐   Drawing ☐

Decorating cakes ☐   Origami ☐

_____

Felix has always dreamed of getting close to a giraffe when he's older. What do you dream of doing when you're older?

Day 21

Date: _____

Draw how you feel today.

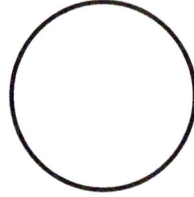

Did you help anyone today? _____

_____

If you could do anything tomorrow, what would it be?

_____

_____

_____

Harper feels really calm when she listens to her favourite music. What helps you to feel calm?

44

Day 22

Date: _____

Use three words to describe today:

      1. _____

      2. _____

      3. _____

Did anything make you anxious today? Draw or write about it here.

What could you do to help someone tomorrow?

_____

Felix absolutely loves spiders and snails! Do you like bugs?

Day 23

Date: _____

Where are you on the happy-o-meter today? Draw a picture of you on the line.

_____

0 - Sad   5 - Ok   10 - Happy

Did anything make you angry today? Draw it here.

How could you be brave tomorrow?

_____
_____
_____
_____

Harper's friend moved away and she really misses her. What could she do to help herself feel better?

Day 24

Date: _____

How does your heart feel today? Write it in the heart shape.

Did anything happen that made you sad today?

_____

_____

Did you notice anyone feeling angry today? How did you know? _____

_____

Felix can't wait to
go bowling tomorrow.
What are you excited
about tomorrow?

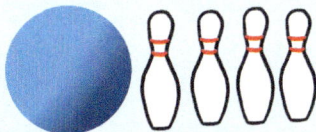

47

DOODLE PAGE

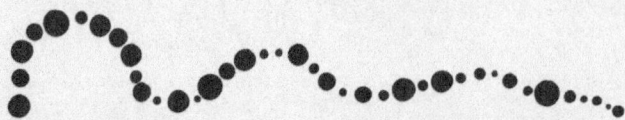

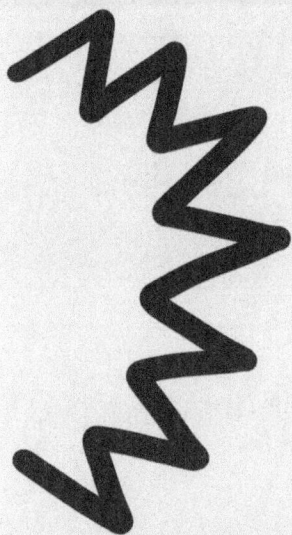

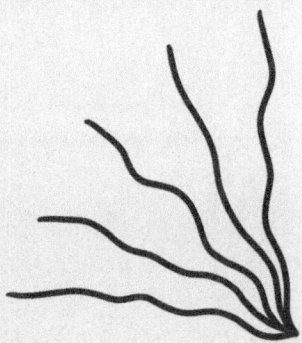

DOODLE PAGE

Day 25

Date: _____

Draw how you feel today.

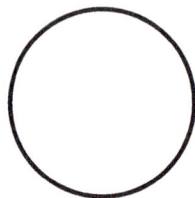

○

Did you have to do something today that you didn't enjoy? _____

_____

Draw what you are looking forward to in the next few days.

Harper feels a bit sad today, but doesn't know why. Do you ever feel like that?

Date: _____

What score would you give today out of 10? _____

What was the best part of today? Draw it here.

Has anyone done anything kind for you today?

_____

_____

_____

Felix has a football match this weekend and is excited and nervous all at once. Can you think of a time you have felt excited and nervous at the same time?

Day 27

Date: _____

Use 3 words to describe today.

_____

_____

_____

Did anything unexpected happen today?

_____
_____
_____

How could you make tomorrow fantastic?

_____
_____
_____

Harper is fascinated by space and would love to meet a real astronaut. Who would you love to meet?

Date: _____

Draw your favourite moment from today.

What did you find hard today?

_____
_____
_____

Is there anything you are anxious about tomorrow?

Meeting new people ☐
Going somewhere new ☐

_____

Felix is feeling anxious about starting swimming lessons next week. What advice would you give him?

Date: _____

Name 3 things you are grateful for today:

_____

_____

_____

Did anything make you angry today? Draw it here.

Think of one person you can be kind to tomorrow.
How will you be kind to them? _____

_____

Harper is feeling very
sad today. What tools can she
use on page 9?

Day 30

Date: _____

Draw a comic strip to show what happened today.

Did anything make you feel calm today?

_____
_____

What could you do to make someone happy tomorrow?

_____
_____
_____
_____

Felix helped his brother with his homework today. How do you think this has made them both feel?

Day 31

Date: _____

Circle all the feelings you have felt today.

Happy   Sad   Anxious   Calm

Other_____   Angry   Excited

Name one thing that went well today, and one thing that could have gone better:

Went well: _____

Could have gone better: _____

Draw two things you're excited about.

Harper is planning to go to the beach in the summer. Do you like visiting the beach?

Date: _____

What was your favourite moment from today?

_____
_____
_____

Did you struggle with anything today? Draw it here.

If you could have dinner with anyone, who would it be?

_____
_____
_____

Felix loves playing board games. What's your favourite game?

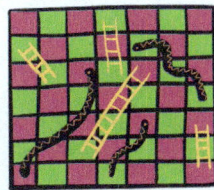

Date: _____

Draw your face on the day-o-meter!

_____

0 1 2 3 4 5 6 7 8 9 10

Worst day!   OK I guess   Best day!

Did anything happen to make you feel anxious today?

_____
_____

How could you encourage someone tomorrow?

_____
_____
_____

Harper has a pet goldfish.
Do you have any pets?

Day 34

Date: _____

Use 3 words to describe today.

1. _____
2. _____
3. _____

What have you learnt today? Draw it here

Did anyone do anything kind for you today?

_____
_____
_____

Felix finds maths really
hard. Do you have to try
hard with any learning?

Day 35

Date: _____

Draw how you feel today. ◯

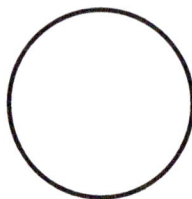

Did anything go really well today? Draw it here.

Think of one person who you could help tomorrow.
Write 3 ways you could help them.
1. _____
2. _____
3. _____

Harper loves inventing
things. If you could create anything,
what would it be?

Day 36

Date: _____

How full is your tank today? Check out page 15 to help you.

Full →

Empty →

What have you found out about yourself today?

_____
_____
_____

Draw something that you're excited about.

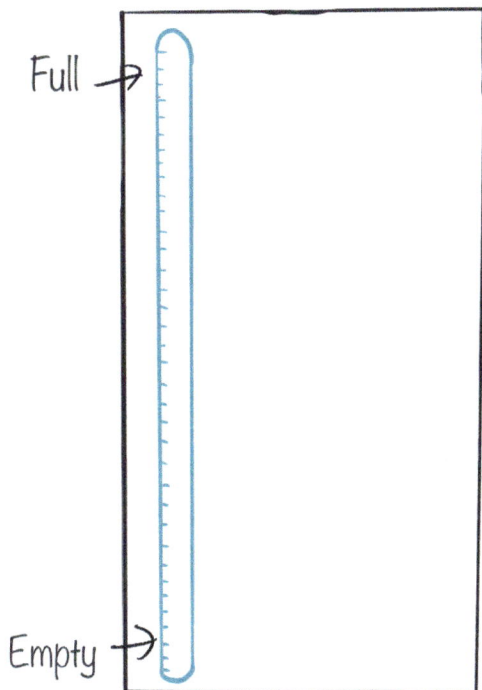

Felix finds it hard to make new friends. What advice could you give him?

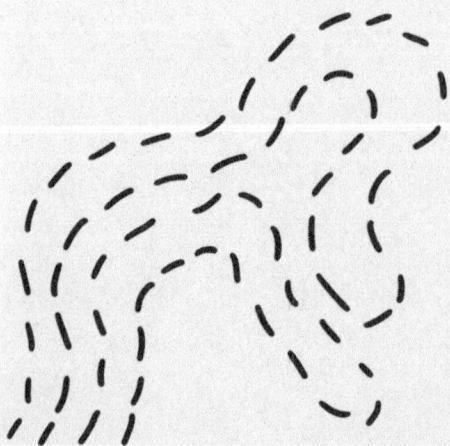

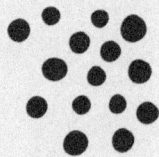

DOODLE PAGE

Day 37

Date: _____

Circle all the feelings you have felt today.

Anxious   Angry   Happy   Excited

                              Calm
Other_____   Sad

What was the hardest thing you did today?

_____

If you could do anything tomorrow, what would it be?
Draw or write it here.

Harper absolutely loves
waking up early and listening to
the birds singing outside her window.
Do you have a favourite
time of day?

Day 38

Date: _____

What was the biggest feeling you felt today?

_____

Draw something you did that helped someone else today.

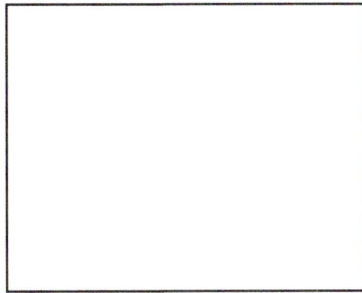

Are you anxious about anything that is happening soon? Write or draw it in the bubble.

Felix told a lie today and got someone else in trouble. What should he do to put it right?

Day 39

Date: _____

How full is your tank feeling today? Draw an arrow on the tank.

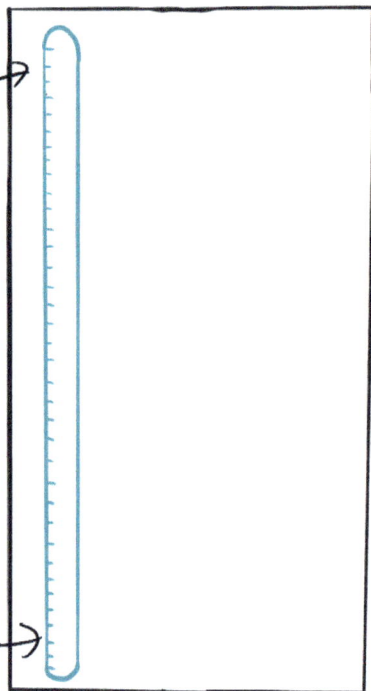

Full →

Empty →

Has anything drained your tank today?

People being mean ☐
Too tired ☐
Finding something hard ☐

_____

What can you do tomorrow to fill up your tank? Draw it here.

Harper gets to choose new glasses today. What colour and pattern would you choose?

Day 40

Date: _____

Describe your day in 3 words:

1. _____
2. _____
3. _____

Has anyone been a good friend to you today? If so, what did they do? _____

_____

What can you do to make sure tomorrow is a calm day? Draw or write it here.

Felix's close friends are funny and kind. What qualities do you look for in a friend?

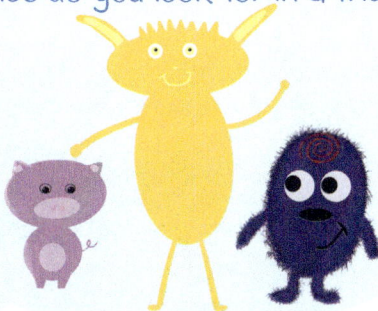

Day 41

Date: _____

Draw your feelings rollercoaster for today.

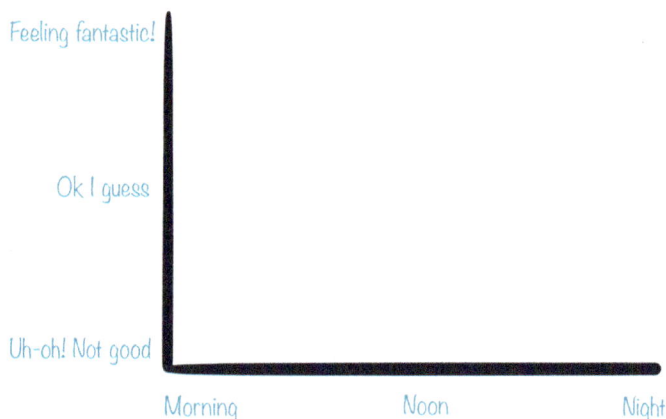

Feeling fantastic!

Ok I guess

Uh-oh! Not good

Morning   Noon   Night

What did you do well today?
_____

If you could redo anything today, what would it be?
_____
_____

Harper tells her mum
and her cousin everything. Who do
you talk to about everything?

68

Day 42

Date: _____

How does your heart feel today? Colour in using the key.

Happy   Angry

Calm

Excited   Anxious

Sad

Did anything happen today that made you happy? Draw or write it here.

One thing I have learnt about myself today is:_____
_____
_____
_____

Felix would love to try snowboarding. What new hobby would you like to try?

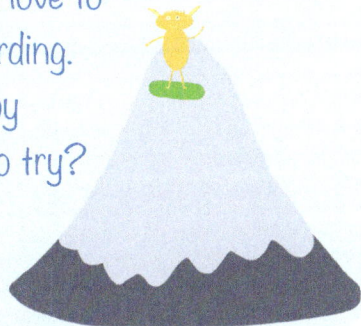

69

Date: _____

Draw how you're feeling today.

What did you have to try really hard at today?

_____
_____
_____

Are you feeling anxious about anything? Which tools from your toolbox can you use to help you?

_____
_____
_____

Harper is really inspired by her neighbour, who paints beautiful pictures. Does anyone inspire you?

Date: _____

In the heart, write down all the feelings you have felt today.

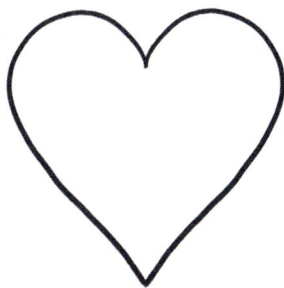

Draw something that made you smile today:

If you could do anything tomorrow, what would it be?

_____

_____

_____

Felix loves telling jokes.
Do you know any
good jokes?

Knock knock...

Day 45

Date: _____

What was the best part of today?

_____

_____

_____

Did you make anyone laugh today?

_____

Has anything made you angry today? How did you deal with it? Draw it here.

Harper would love
to meet the Queen!
Who would you like to meet?

Date: _____

Draw in the faces on the mood tracker to show how you were feeling at each part of the day.

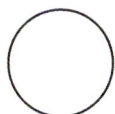 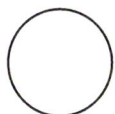 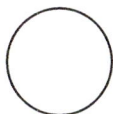 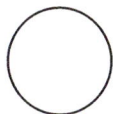

Get up   Lunch   Dinner   Bed

Did you see anyone who was sad or angry today? How could you tell?_____

_____

What did you do today to take care of yourself?

Read a book ☐
Drew a picture ☐
Watched favourite movie ☐
Went to the park ☐

_____

_____

_____

Felix loves sewing, and has recently made outfits for his teddy bear. What do you like to make?

73

Date: _____

Use 2 words to describe today:

_____

What did you do today that was creative? Draw it here.

How could you help someone tomorrow?

Empty dishwasher ☐
Play with sibling ☐
Wash up ☐
Tidy up ☐

_____

Harper needs to buy a present for her mum. What could she get her?

Day 48

Date: _____

Score today out of 10 _____

Did anything surprise you today? If so, draw it here.

If you could redo any part of today, what would you do differently? _____

_____

Felix really wants to go to a friend's party tomorrow, but he is meant to be helping out at home. What should he do?

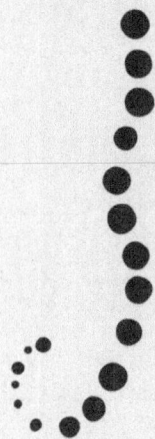

Day 49

Date: _____

Circle all the feelings you have felt today.

Anxious

Happy

Angry

Excited

Other_____

Sad

Calm

Did anything make you sad today? Draw or write it here.

When something makes me anxious I can... _____

_____

_____

_____

Harper hasn't seen her auntie for ages and really misses her. Do you miss anyone that you haven't seen for a long time?

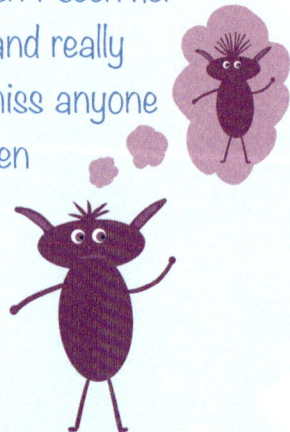

Day 50

Date: _____

What was the best part about today?

_____
_____
_____

What have you done today to keep yourself calm?
Counted to 10 ☐
Talked to a friend ☐
Listened to music ☐

_____

Draw something you are excited about in the future.

Felix is feeling sad about something that happened at school. What advice can you give him?

Day 51

Date: _____

Describe your day in 5 words:

_____
_____
_____

What was the kindest thing you heard someone say today? Write it in the bubble.

One thing I have learnt today is _____

_____

_____

Harper loves creating stories with whimsical characters. Do you like dreaming up stories?

80

Day 52

Date: _____

Draw 3 things you are grateful for today.

Did anything worry you today?

_____
_____
_____

If you could time travel, when would you go to?

_____

Felix is fascinated by the lifecycle of a butterfly. Do you enjoy learning about nature?

Date: _____

What's the biggest feeling you have felt today?

_____

What are you most proud of yourself for today?
Draw it here.

Did anything go wrong today? How did you feel?

_____
_____
_____

Harper really wants to go
canoeing with her school, but is feeling
really anxious about it. What should she do?

Date: _____

Something that went really well today was...

_____

_____

_____

Something that didn't go so well today was...

_____

_____

_____

Draw one thing you hope to do tomorrow.

Felix is really good
at crosswords. Are you?

Day 55

Date: _____

Write 3 good things that happened today.

_____
_____
_____

Draw something that made you laugh today.

When I am finding something hard I will:

Keep trying ☐
Ask for help ☐
Give up ☐

_____

_____

Harper is angry with
her little brother. What
tools can she use from the
anger tool box? (pg 7)

Date: _____

Choose 3 letters. Now think of 3 good things that happened today, starting with those letters.

1. _____

2. _____

3. _____

What was the most difficult part of today?

_____

_____

What could you do to fill up your tank tomorrow?
(check out pg 15)

Felix is good at
basketball but he wants to get better
so he can join a team. How can he improve?

Date: _____

Draw how you feel today, on the face.

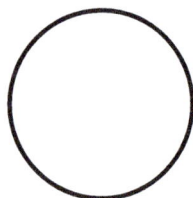

Have you learnt anything new about yourself today?

_____
_____
_____

Did you notice anyone with big feelings today?
What did you do?

Talked to them ☐
Told a teacher ☐
Stayed with them ☐
Offered them a tissue ☐

_____

Harper had an argument with her mum and now feels bad. What can she do?

Date: _____

What was your favourite moment from today? Draw or write it here.

What do you know today that you didn't know yesterday? _____
_____
_____

How are you feeling about tomorrow? What is making you feel that way? _____
_____

Felix was really surprised
to learn his Mum and Dad sometimes
feel anxious and sad too. Do you think the grown
ups in your life ever feel like this?

Day 59

Date: _____

Where are you on the happy-o-meter today?

_____

0 - Sad   5 - Ok   10 - Happy

What was the most exciting part of today?

_____
_____
_____

Who could you help tomorrow? Write their name in the bubble and decorate it.

Going to the aquarium helps Harper feel calm. What helps you feel calm?

88

Date:_____

How does your heart feel today? Colour it in using the key:

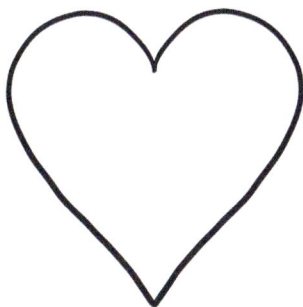

Happy   Angry   Calm   Excited   Anxious   Sad

Full →

Did anything make you sad today? _____
_____
_____

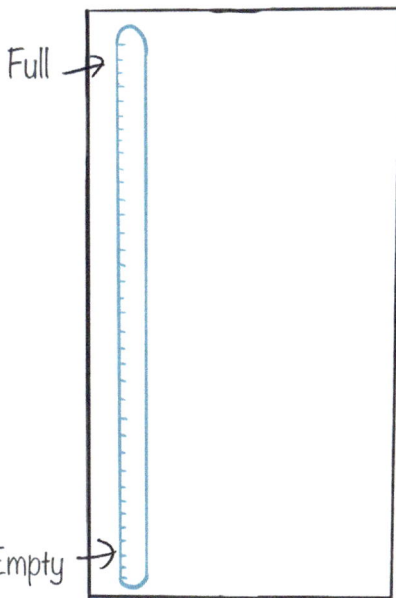

Empty →

Felix is so happy about having a new baby cousin. What has made you happy today?

How can you fill up your tank tomorrow? Write the words in the tank.

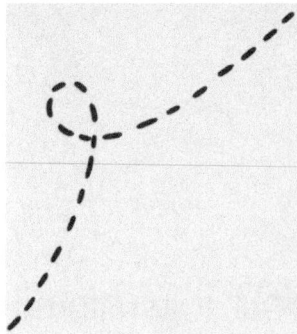

DOODLE PAGE

DOODLE PAGE

Printed in Great Britain
by Amazon